ENGLISH
INTERPLAY

Also by Raymond C. Clark:

The ESL Miscellany
Getting a Fix on Vocabulary
More Index Card Games
Match It!
Living in the United States
Story Cards: Aesop's Fables
Story Cards: Tales of Nasreddin Hodja

ENGLISH INTERPLAY

SURVIVING

RAYMOND C. CLARK

Illustrations by Nancy Shrewsbury Nadel

PRO LINGUA ⊙ **ASSOCIATES**

Pro Lingua Associates, Publishers
P.O.Box 1348
Brattleboro, Vermont 05302 USA
Office: 802 257 7779
Orders: 800 366 4775
Fax: 802 257 5117
E-mail: prolingu@sover.net
Webstore: WWW. ProLinguaAssociates.com
SAN: 216-0579

*At **Pro Lingua**
our objective is to foster
an approach to learning and teaching
that we call **interplay**, the **inter**action of language
learners and teachers with their materials, with
the language and culture, and with
each other in active, creative
and productive **play**.*

ISBN 0-86647-155-3

This book was set in a font called Times New Roman and Arial Rounded display type. The cover and illustrations are by Nancy Shrewsbury Nadel. The book was designed by the author and Arthur A. Burrows. It was printed and bound by Capital City Press in Montpelier, Vermont.

Printed in the United States of America
First printing 2002. There are 3,000 copies in print.

Contents

WELCOME
TO
INTERPLAY ENGLISH

LESSON ONE

1.1 THIS IS _____'S BOOK

MY TEACHER IS _____

MY SCHEDULE

DAY	CLASS	TIME	PLACE

GOOD MORNING.	GOOD MORNING. HOW ARE YOU?
FINE, THANK YOU. HOW ARE YOU?	FINE, THANKS.

GOOD AFTERNOON.	GOOD AFTERNOON.
HOW ARE YOU.	I'M FINE. HOW ARE YOU?
NOT BAD.	

GOOD EVENING.	GOOD EVENING. HOW ARE YOU?
GOOD. HOW ARE YOU?	GOOD.

THE ALPHABET

A B C D E F G

H I J K L M N O P

Q R S T U V

W X Y Z

a b c d e f g

h i j k l m n o p

q r s t u v w x y z

A B C D E F G

H I J K L M N O P

Q R S T U V

W X Y Z

a b c d e f g

h i j k l m n o p

q r s t u v w x y z

A   HELLO. MY NAME IS _____ .

I AM YOUR TEACHER.

YOU ARE MY STUDENTS.

PLEASE CALL ME _____ .

B   WHAT IS YOUR NAME?   MY NAME IS _____ .

PLEASE CALL ME _____ .

C   WHERE ARE YOU FROM?   I AM FROM _____ .

MY CLASS

_____   _____

_____   _____

_____   _____

_____   _____

_____   _____

_____   _____

_____   _____

_____   _____

_____   _____

_____   _____

_____   _____

_____   _____

1.5   ASK AND ANSWER

WHAT IS THE NAME OF THIS LETTER?
(WHAT'S)

IT IS   _____.
(IT'S)

A   E   I   O   U

B   C   D   G   P   T   V   Z

F   L   M   N   S   X

J   K   H

Q   W

R   Y

1.6   POINT AND ASK

EXCUSE ME.   CAN I HELP YOU?
PLEASE SAY THIS.   IT'S _____.
                                   (IT IS)

THANK YOU.   YOU'RE WELCOME.
                                   (YOU ARE)

A	G	L	M	Q	R
E	P	D	Z	Y	U
I	B	F	G	H	S
O	C	J	N	K	T
U	V	X	Z	W	A

1.7 POINT, ASK, AND SAY

HOW DO YOU SAY THIS?   IT'S _____.
(IT IS)

b	m	r	t	s	w
p	c	a	d	z	e
x	y	d	l	e	j
i	n	q	f	o	k
g	u	v	h	z	d
w	o	r	t	i	s

1.8 LET'S PRACTICE — LOOK AND SAY

N - A - M - E	M - Y	T - E - A - C - H - E - R
S - T - U - D - E - N - T - S	A - M	I
H - E - L - L - O	I - S	Y - O - U - R
Y - O - U	A - R - E	C - A - L - L

1.9 SAY

I SPELL MY FIRST NAME   __ __ __ __ __ __ __ __ __ __ .

I SPELL MY LAST NAME   __ __ __ __ __ __ __ __ __ __ __.

PLEASE SPELL YOUR NAME.

            I SPELL MY FIRST NAME   __ __ __ __ __ __.

            I SPELL MY LAST NAME   __ __ __ __ __ __.

YOU SPELL YOUR NAME   __ __ __ __ __.

IS THAT RIGHT?   YES IT IS.
                  NO IT ISN'T.

1.10 WRITE

HELLO. M_____   N_____   I___   _____   _____.

I A___ Y_____ S_____.

Y____   A_____   M_____ T_____.

P_____   C_____   M___ _____.

W_____ I___ Y_____ N_____?

M____ N_____ I___ _____   _____.

1.11 SAY, LISTEN, AND DO

PLEASE GO TO THE BOARD.

GO SLOWLY.

WHAT ARE YOU DOING?   I AM GOING TO THE BOARD.

WHAT IS HE/SHE DOING?   HE/SHE IS GOING TO THE BOARD.

NOW WRITE YOUR NAME.
GOOD. WHAT ARE YOU DOING?   I AM WRITING MY NAME.

WHAT IS HE/SHE DOING?   HE/SHE IS WRITING HIS/HER NAME.

PLEASE GO BACK TO YOUR SEAT.
WHAT ARE YOU DOING?   I AM GOING BACK TO MY SEAT.

ON THE STREET

I'M SORRY. I DON'T UNDERSTAND. PLEASE SPEAK SLOWLY.
MY ENGLISH IS NOT VERY GOOD.

1.12 LISTEN AND SAY

HERE IS YOUR HOMEWORK.
DO IT AT HOME.
PLEASE BRING IT BACK.

CLASS IS OVER.   LET'S GO HOME.
SEE YOU LATER.   SEE YOU LATER.
GOODBYE CLASS.   GOODBYE TEACHER.

WORDS

ANSWER	EXCUSE	PRACTICE
ASK	GO	SAY
BE (AM, ARE, IS)	HELP	SEE
BRING	LET	SPEAK
CALL	LISTEN	SPELL
CAN	LOOK	UNDERSTAND
DO	POINT	WRITE

AFTERNOON	HOME	SCHEDULE
ALPHABET	HOMEWORK	SEAT
AND	HOW	SLOWLY
AT	LAST	SORRY
BACK	LATER	STREET
BAD	LESSON	STUDENT
BOOK	LETTER	TEACHER
BOARD	MORNING	THANKS
CLASS	NAME	THE
CLASSMATE	NO	THAT
DAY	NOT	THIS
ENGLISH	NOW	TIME
EVENING	OF	TO
FINE	ON	VERY
FIRST	ONE	WELCOME
FROM	OVER	WHAT
GOOD	PAGE	WHERE
GOODBYE	PLACE	WORD
HELLO	PLEASE	YES
HERE	RIGHT	

GRAMMAR

TO BE	
I AM	WE ARE
YOU ARE	YOU ARE
HE SHE IS IT	THEY ARE

I AM = I'M	WE ARE = WE'RE
YOU ARE = YOU'RE	YOU ARE = YOU'RE
HE IS = HE'S SHE IS = SHE'S IT IS = IT'S	THEY ARE = THEY'RE
I AM NOT = I'M NOT	WE ARE NOT = WE AREN'T
YOU ARE NOT = YOU AREN'T	YOU ARE NOT = YOU AREN'T
HE IS NOT = HE ISN'T SHE IS NOT = SHE ISN'T IT IS NOT = IT ISN'T	THEY ARE NOT = THEY AREN'T

+	-	?
I AM GOING YOU ARE GOING HE/SHE/IT IS GOING	I AM NOT GOING YOU ARE NOT GOING HE/SHE/IT IS NOT GOING	AM I GOING ARE YOU GOING IS HE/SHE/IT GOING

I	ME	MY	MINE
YOU	YOU	YOUR	YOURS
HE	HIM	HIS	HIS
SHE	HER	HER	HERS
IT	IT	ITS	ITS
WE	US	OUR	OURS
THEY	THEM	THEIR	THEIRS

I CAN HELP **YOU** DO **YOUR** HOMEWORK.
MINE IS HERE. IS THIS **YOURS**?

LESSON 2 (TWO)

2.1   LOOK, LISTEN, READ, AND SAY

HE IS A PERSON.

SHE IS A PERSON

THEY ARE PEOPLE.

HE IS A MAN.

THEY ARE MEN.

SHE IS A WOMAN.

THEY ARE WOMEN.

HE IS A CHILD.   SHE IS A CHILD.   THEY ARE CHILDREN.

HE IS A BOY.   THEY ARE BOYS.

SHE IS A GIRL.   THEY ARE GIRLS.

IT IS A BABY.   THEY ARE BABIES.

2.2   ASK QUESTIONS AND ANSWER WITH YES OR NO

EXAMPLES: Is he a man?   Yes, he is.
    or   Is he a woman?   No, he isn't. He's a man.

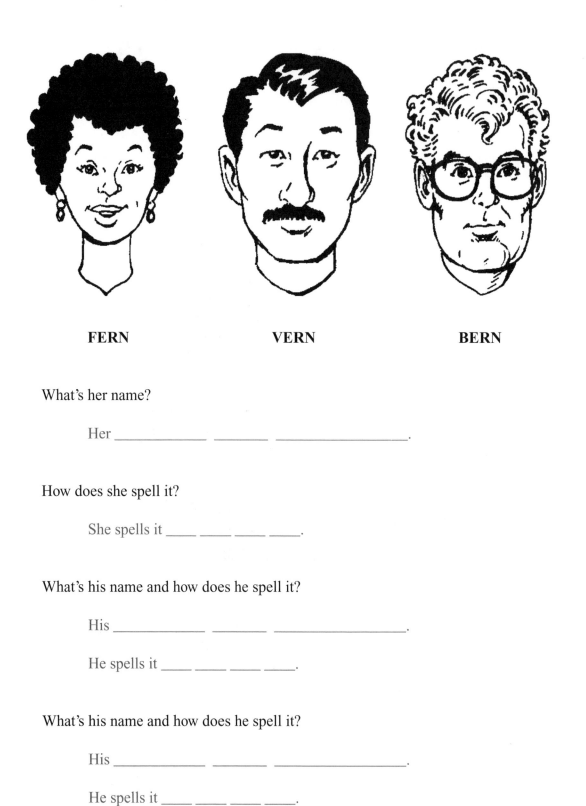

FERN   **VERN**   **BERN**

What's her name?

Her _____ _____ _____.

How does she spell it?

She spells it ____ ____ ____ ____.

What's his name and how does he spell it?

His _____ _____ _____.

He spells it ____ ____ ____ ____.

What's his name and how does he spell it?

His _____ _____ _____.

He spells it ____ ____ ____ ____.

BETH **BESS** **BETTE**

What are their names and how do they spell them?

Their _____ _____ _____, _____, _____.

They _____ their _____ ____ ____ ____ ____, ____ ____ ____ ____,

and ____ ____ ____ ____ ____.

2.4 READ, WRITE, AND SAY

How do you and _____ spell your names?

We _____ _____ _____ ____ ____ ____ ____ ____

and ____ ____ ____ ____ ____ ____ ____.

How do _____ and _____ spell their names?

They _____ _____ _____ ____ ____ ____ ____

and ____ ____ ____ ____ ____ ____ ____.

His name is Chuck.

These people are his friends.

Eve

Bert

Brooke

Jill

Gus

Ruth

Jane

Mike

Zoey

Jeff

Howie

Joe

Max

Jon

Paul

His dog is **Dotcom.**   His cat is **Queenie.**

Who's this?
(Who is)

It's _____.

EXAMPLE:

Is this Queenie?   Yes, it is.

Is this Jeff?   No, it isn't.
                                            (is not)
                                        It's Bert.

NOW ASK ABOUT CHUCK'S FRIENDS.

EVE	JILL	JANE	JEFF	MAX
he	is	say	get	cat
green	it	make	red	at
seat	this	wait	tell	bad
queen	did	gray	head	am
here	his	name	friend	black

BERT	GUS	MIKE	HOWIE	JON
her	fun	my	down	not
word	some	try	town	stop
first	run	child	now	hot
fur	come	high	how	got
heard	one	write	out	far

BROOKE	RUTH	ZOEY	JOE	PAUL
pull	do	boy	no	ball
good	school	toy	slow	law
put	new	oil	show	walk
look	rule	spoil	boat	saw
would	blue	noise	hole	taught

2.9   READ AND SAY

__ L	blink	clink	fling	glint	plink	slim
__ R	bring	cringe	drink	grin	shrink	fringe	prince	trim
__ W	quick	swim	twin
S __	skim	slim	smith	snip	spill	still	swim
S __ __	script	split	spring	squish	string

2.10 READ AND SAY

Where's Jon?

Jon's here.

Where's Gus?

Gus's there.

Where are Jon and Bert.

Where are Gus and Ruth?

They're here.
(They are)

They're there.

ASK AND ANSWER

_____, where are you and _____?
(name)   We're here.

_____, where are _____ and _____?
                                                      They're there.

_____, where are _____ and _____?

_____'s here

and _____'s there.

2.11 READ AND SAY

Colors here and colors there.
Every color everywhere.
Red and orange, pink and blue,
Yellow, green, and purple, too.

Black and white, gray and brown.
Colors everywhere in the town.
Colors here and colors there.
Every color everywhere.

2.12   LISTEN, SAY, AND DO

Do you have your homework?   Yes, I do.
                                           No, I don't.

Do all of you have your homework?   Yes, we do.
                                           No, we don't.

Good. Please give it to me.   Here you are.

What are you doing?   I'm giving my homework to you.

What is he/she doing?   He/She's giving his/her homework to you.

2.13   ASK AND ANSWER: A CARD GAME

A What do you have?   I have one/two/three _____ cards.

B Do you have a/any _____?   Yes, I do have a/some _____.
                                                        or
                                           No, I don't have a/any _____.

May I have him/her/it/them?

ON THE STREET

Excuse me. Where can I find a bathroom?

NEW WORDS

find	have	read
give	may	repeat
a	everywere	question
about	example	red
all	friend	there
any	game	these
baby	gray	three
bathroom	green	too
black	girl	town
blue	in	two
boy	man/men	where
brown	new	white
card	or	who
cat	orange	with
child/children	person/people	woman/women
color	pink	yellow
dog	pronunciation	
every	purple	

PRONUNCIATION

/s/	/z/	/iz/
books	dogs	classes
cats	lessons	pages
seats	names	places
streets	teachers	
students	words	

GRAMMAR

+	−	?
I AM	I AM NOT	AM I
HE SHE IS IT	HE SHE IS NOT IT (ISN'T)	HE IS SHE IT
WE YOU ARE THEY	WE YOU ARE NOT THEY (AREN'T)	WE ARE YOU THEY

TO HAVE

I HAVE	WE HAVE
YOU HAVE	YOU HAVE
HE SHE HAS IT	THEY HAVE

+	−	?	WH ?
I HAVE	I DO NOT HAVE (DON'T)	DO I HAVE	WHAT DO I HAVE
SHE HAS	SHE DOES NOT HAVE (DOESN'T)	DOES SHE HAVE	WHAT DOES SHE HAVE

QUESTION WORDS

WHO   WHAT   WHERE   HOW

LESSON 3

3.1 LISTEN AND SAY

Did you bring your homework?   Yes I/we did.
Please hand in your homework.
What are you doing?   I'm handing in my homework.
Thank you. You handed in your homework.
What did you do?   I/we handed in my/our homework.
Was it easy or difficult?   It was (very) easy/difficult.

3.2A LOOK, LISTEN, AND READ

0
zero

1   **2**   **3**
one   **two**   **three**

4   **5**   **6**
four   **five**   **six**

7   **8**   **9**
seven   **eight**   **nine**

10   **11**   **12**
ten   **eleven**   **twelve**

3.2B SAY, SPELL, AND WRITE

FOR EXAMPLE: ℍℍ   <u>Five,   F - I - V - E,   5</u>

III	_____	IIII	_____
ℍℍ II	_____	ℍℍ III	_____
I	_____	ℍℍ ℍℍ II	_____
III	_____	II	_____
ℍℍ I	_____	ℍℍ ℍℍ	_____
ℍℍ ℍℍ I	_____	ℍℍ IIII	_____

3.3   LOOK, SAY, READ, AND WRITE

How much is this?
EXAMPLE: $2 + 7 =$ Two and seven is nine.

$1 + 8 =$ _____ $4 + 5 =$ _____

$3 + 3 =$ _____ $4 + 2 =$ _____

$7 + 3 =$ _____ $5 + 6 =$ _____

$7 + 5 =$ _____ $2 + 6 =$ _____

$8 + 4 =$ _____ $9 + 1 =$ _____

$10 + 2 =$ _____ $8 + 3 =$ _____

$7 + 5 =$ _____ $10 + 1 =$ _____

3.4   READ AND SAY

My day begins at seven.
I work from nine to five.
My lunch is twelve to one,
  sometimes from one to two.
I'm home at ten to six,
  and pretty tired, too.

I watch TV at eight,
  on channels three or four.
At ten it is quite late.
I go and lock the door,
  and then it is eleven.
My day begins at seven.

Excuse me, teacher, I don't know this word.
What does _____ mean?

Now do you understand?

Yes, I do.
No, I don't.

OK, look it up in your dictionary.

bucks   lottery   choose   win   lose   drawing

ticket   collect   fold   piece   number

BIG BUCKS LOTTERY

N	1	3	5	8	11
U	4	6	9	10	12
M	1	2	7	8	11
B	2	4	6	9	10
E	2	5	7	8	11
R	2	4	7	9	12
S	3	5	6	10	12

3.6   LISTEN AND LOOK

SAY THE TICKET NUMBERS
NOW CHOOSE ONE TICKET.

Example:

The winning ticket is E - 2 - 5 - 7 - 8 -11.

Who has the winning ticket?	I do.
Who won?	_____ did.
Read your ticket number, please.	It's __ __ __ __ __.
Who lost?	I did.
Who has a losing ticket?	I do.
What ticket did you have?	I had __ __ __ __ __.
How many winning numbers did you have?	I had _____.

3.7   LISTEN, DO, AND SAY

A   Take a pen or pencil and a piece of paper.

Write five numbers on it.

What are you doing?	I'm writing five numbers.
Fold the paper.	
Wait! What are you going to do?	I'm going to fold the paper.
Go ahead.	
_____, please collect all the tickets.	
What's _____ doing?	He/she's collecting all the tickets.
Now give the tickets to me.	
Now tell me what happened.	I took, wrote, folded
	_____ collected, gave

B   OK, now listen.

Here's the winning number: __ __ __ __ __.

Who wrote it?	I did!

3.8   LISTEN AND SAY

Let's take a break.	OK! How long?
Take ten minutes, but don't be late.	Don't worry.
	We'll be back in eight.

3.9 LISTEN AND WRITE

My teacher's telephone number is _____.
The area code here is (   ).

3.10 ASK AND ANSWER

_____, what's your telephone number?

It's _____.

Would you please say that again?   Sure, It's _____.
Thanks.

MY CLASSMATE'S TELEPHONE NUMBERS

PERSON	AREA CODE	NUMBER
_____	_____	_____
_____	_____	_____
_____	_____	_____
_____	_____	_____
_____	_____	_____
_____	_____	_____
_____	_____	_____
_____	_____	_____
_____	_____	_____

0 = zero = oh

3.11   LISTEN AND LOOK

This is a map of the United States, Canada, and Mexico. They are countries.
Ontario is a province in Canada. Ontario is a big province.
Delaware is a little state in the United States. The United States has 50 states.
Canada has eleven provinces. Mexico has 31 states.

3.12 SAY

AL 35203	GA 30304	MD 21233	PA 19104	UT 84199
BC V8V 4V2	HI 96820	NB E2L 5L4	PQ H2Y 3B3	VA 22314
CA 90210	IL 60045	NJ 07101	RI 02904	VT 05301
DE 19850	KY 40231	NY 10029	SC 29292	WA 98109
DC 20066	LA 70113	OH 43216	TN 38101	WY 82001
FL 32203	MA 01376	ON N2J 3Z9	TX 77201	ZIP

Our zip code is _____.

Our state/province is _____.

3.13 LISTEN AND WRITE

EVERY DAY

Her day _____ at seven.
She _____ from nine to five.
Her lunch is twelve to one,
   sometimes from one to two.
She _____ home at ten to six,
   and pretty tired, too.
She _____ TV at eight,
   on channels three or four.
At ten it is quite late.
She _____ and _____ the door,
   and then it is eleven.
Her day _____ at seven.

YESTERDAY

Her day _____ at seven.
She _____ from nine to five.
Her lunch _____ twelve to one,
   or _____ it one to two?
She _____ home at ten to six,
   and pretty tired, too.
She _____ TV at eight,
   on channels three or four.
At ten it _____ quite late.
She _____ and _____ the door,
   and then it _____ eleven.
Her day _____ at seven.

Class is over.   Let's go home.

But wait! I almost forgot.

Here's your homework.

_____ and _____,

  will you hand it out?

What are you doing?

What are they doing?

That's all for today.

Have a nice day.

ON THE STREET

Is this seat taken?
May I sit here?

NEW WORDS

begin	happen	wait
be going to	know	watch
choose	lock	will
collect	look up	win
fold	lose	work
forget	mean	worry
hand in	sit	would
hand out	take	

again	from	pretty
ahead	late	province
almost	little	quite
area code	long	seven
big	lottery	six
break	lunch	sometimes
buck	many	state
but	map	sure
channel	minute	telephone
country	much	ten
dictionary	nice	then
difficult	nine	ticket
door	number	tired
easy	OK	TV
eight	paper	twelve
eleven	pen	yesterday
five	pencil	zero
four	piece	zip code

PRONUNCIATION

/s/	/z/	/iz/
works	begins	watches
locks	goes	chooses
collects	folds	loses
takes	knows	
waits	wins	

GRAMMAR

BE GOING TO	
I am going to go	We are going to go
You are going to go	You are going to go
He She is going to go It	They are going to go

begin—began
bring—brought
choose—chose
find—found
give—gave
go—went

have—had
know—knew
lose—lost
read—read
say—said
speak—spoke

take—took
understand—understood
win—won
write—wrote

look— looked
lock—locked
watch—watched
work—worked
ask—asked
help—helped

worry—worried
answer—answered
call—called
listen—listened
spell—spelled
point—pointed

collect—collected
fold—folded
hand—handed
wait—waited
repeat—repeated

+	–	?	WH ?
I had	I did not have	Did I have	What did I have
You won	You did not win	Did you win	What did you win
She lost	She did not lose	Did she lose	What did she lose
He wrote	He did not write	Did he write	What did he write
It brought	It did not bring	Did it bring	What did it bring
We went	We did not go	Did we go	Where did we go
They gave	They did not give	Did they give	What did they give

did not = didn't

B I N G O

Card 20			
16	17	14	90
15	70	80	30
13	12	50	40
18	19	60	20

Card 30			
12	14	15	13
70	80	17	60
90	50	30	18
16	40	19	20

Card 40			
14	19	15	20
17	16	80	18
30	12	13	40
50	70	60	90

Card 50			
13	15	17	80
60	14	30	16
18	20	70	90
50	19	40	12

Card 60			
18	60	15	90
17	30	20	50
13	80	14	12
16	40	19	70

Card 70			
70	12	40	13
20	15	80	16
14	50	18	90
16	17	19	30

Card 80			
12	50	90	14
18	20	40	17
16	60	30	13
15	19	70	80

Card 90			
60	18	20	12
80	40	14	13
70	19	30	50
15	90	16	17

4.1   LISTEN, REPEAT AND WRITE

13 _____   30 _____

14 _____   40 _____

15 _____   50 _____

16 _____   60 _____

17 _____   70 _____

18 _____   80 _____

19 _____   90 _____

20 _____

4.2   LET'S PLAY BINGO!

First, choose one card.

Which card have you chosen?   I've chosen card number _____.

Now, when I say a number, make an
X on the number.

When you have four in a row, across,
 up, or down, say Bingo.

What will you say?   I'll say bingo.

When will you say it?   When I have four in a row, across, up, or down.

Are you ready?   Ready.

Let's go.

                                           Bingo!

Please read your numbers.

Let's play another game.

Choose a different card.

A

13¢	14 USA Julia Ward Howe	15¢	16¢
			Rachel Carson USA 17c
18¢	USA 19c Sequoyah	20¢	Mary Cassatt USA 23
			25¢
31¢	EDITOR Henry R. Luce USA 32	35¢	45¢
			Chester W. Nimitz USA 50
56¢	58¢	H.H.'Hap'Arnold USA 65	68¢
			70¢
72¢	74¢	75¢	Mary Breckinridge USA 77
			78¢

Do you have a _____ cent stamp?   Yes, I do. Do you want it?

Yes I do. Who's on the _____ cent stamp?   _____.

Can you spell his/her last name?   Do I have to?

Yes, you do.   All right. It's ___ ___ ___ ___ ___ ___   ___ ___ ___.

Do you have a _____ cent stamp?   No, I don't.

You don't? I don't either.   So, neither of us has a _____ cent stamp.

B

USA 13c Crazy Horse	14¢	Buffalo Bill Cody USA 15	16¢ 17¢
George Mason USA 18c	19¢	Ralph Bunche USA 20c	23¢ Jack London USA 25
31¢	32¢	Dennis Chavez USA 35	45¢ 50¢
John Harvard USA 56	58¢	65¢	68¢ 70¢
72¢	74¢	Wendell Willkie Statesman 75 USA	77¢ Alice Paul SUFFRAGIST USA 78

Do you have a _____ cent stamp?   Yes, I do. Do you want it?

Yes I do. Who's on the _____ cent stamp?   _____.

Can you spell his/her last name?   Do I have to?

Yes, you do.   All right. It's ___ ___ ___ ___ ___ ___ ___ ___ ___.

Do you have a _____ cent stamp?   No, I don't.

You don't? I don't either.   So, neither of us has a _____ cent stamp.

4.4   LISTEN AND SAY

How much is this?

100	=	a hundred
1,000	=	a thousand
1,000,000	=	a million

127	=	one hundred (and) twenty seven
850	=	eight hundred (and) fifty
1,200	=	one thousand two hundred
4,650	=	four thousand six hundred (and) fifty
11, 875	=	eleven thousand eight hundred (and) seventy five
101,000	=	one hundred (and) one thousand
575,000	=	five hundred seventy five thousand
853, 456	=	eight hundred fifty three thousand four hundred (and) fifty six
1,000,000	=	one million
10,000,000	=	ten million

4.5   ASK AND ANSWER

What do you have to do to make a lot of money?

You have to _____,
but you don't have to _____.
Do you agree?

Yes I do/No I don't.

find a job	buy a new TV	work hard
buy a new car	save money	pay the rent
buy new clothes	buy food	learn English
pay taxes	collect stamps	play the lottery
buy a house	rent an apartment	have good friends

4.6 SAY AND WRITE

Example: Ten and three is thirteen.

20 + 13 = _____   120 + 15 = _____

20 + 17 = _____   100 + 40 = _____

20 + 15 = _____   210 + 25 = _____

20 + 18 = _____   450 + 50 = _____

20 + 14 = _____   630 + 300 = _____

20 + 16 = _____   470 + 20 = _____

20 + 12 = _____   510 + 90 = _____

20 + 11 = _____   700 + 110 = _____

20 + 19 = _____   900 + 60 = _____

4.7 SAY AND WRITE

Example: Is this right or wrong?   18 + 17 = 35   That's right.
                                      20 + 10 = 40   That's wrong. It should be 30.

21 + 5 = 26   700 + 250 = 980

130 + 13 = 143   45 + 19 = 54

117 + 3 = 150   600 + 25 = 625

80 + 15 = 105   85 + 12 = 97

250 + 16 = 266   123 + 16 = 138

WRITE, SAY, AND ANSWER

____ + ____ = ____   ____ + ____ = ____

____ + ____ = ____   ____ + ____ = ____

____ + ____ = ____   ____ + ____ = ____

____ + ____ = ____   ____ + ____ = ____

____ + ____ = ____   ____ + ____ = ____

____ + ____ = ____   ____ + ____ = ____

4.8 LISTEN AND ASK

Which one is correct, a or b? Circle the correct number.

I'm sorry. I didn't get that.
Would you say it again, please.

Sure. I said _____.

A	B	A	B	A	B	A	B
14	40	17	70	113	130	116	160
15	50	18	80	114	140	117	170
16	60	19	90	115	150	119	190

4.9 LISTEN AND ASK: PRACTICE IN PAIRS

A	B	A	B
1,200	1,020	105,280	105,218
10,500	10,050	880,900	818,900
15,575	15,570	999,999	999,919
18,210	18,211	19,000,000	90,000,000
20,615	20,650	1,215,000	1,250,000
100,200	120,000	3,618,000	3,680,000

4.10 LISTEN, DO, AND SAY

Take a piece of paper.
What have you just done?   I have just taken a piece of paper.
Write your name on the paper.
What are you doing?
What have you just done?   I have just written my name.
Write six numbers on the paper.
Say the numbers.
What have you just done?   I have just said the numbers.
Throw away the paper.
What have you done?   I have thrown away the paper.
Now tell me everything you
    have done up to now.
Now tell me what you did on page 25.

How much is the _____?

I would say it is worth _____.

• That's correct. You have just won _____, worth _____.
• Sorry, that's incorrect. Guess again.

1999 Buick
$16,997

$4,997
1995
Jeep Grand Cherokee

$19,997
2001
Isuzu Trooper

1995 Dodge Neon
$2,497

$26,197
2002 Chevy Tahoe

2002 Toyota Sienna Wagon
$22,497

2000 Olds Silouette
$19,997

1994 Isuzu Trooper
$7,997

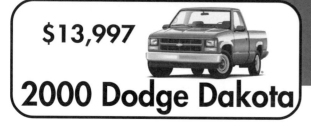

$13,997
2000 Dodge Dakota

1999 Toyota Camry
$11,297

NEW WORDS

agree	get	pay	tell
buy	guess	play	throw away
circle	have to	save	want
	learn	send	
	make	should	

across	different	money	tax
all right	down	neither	thousand
another	either	pair	up
apartment	food	postage	up to now
Bingo	house	ready	verb
car	hundred	rent	when
cent	job	row	which
clothes	just	so	worth
(in)correct	million	stamp	wrong

ON THE STREET

I want to send this to Siberia.
How much is the postage?

GRAMMAR

VERBS		
I	CAN MAY SHOULD WILL WOULD HAVE TO AM GOING TO	GO

EVERY DAY	NOW (AM/ARE/IS + ING)	YESTERDAY	JUST NOW (HAVE/HAS + EN/D/T)
begin(s)	beginning	began	begun
bring(s)	bringing	brought	brought
buy(s)	buying	bought	bought
choose(s)	choosing	chose	chosen
do(es)	doing	did	done
find(s)	finding	found	found
forget(s)	forgetting	forgot	forgotten
get(s)	getting	got	gotten
give(s)	giving	gave	given
go(es)	going	went	gone
have/has	having	had	had
know(s)	knowing	knew	known
lose(s)	losing	lost	lost
make(s)	making	made	made
mean(s)	meaning	meant	meant
pay(s)	paying	paid	paid
read(s)	reading	read	read
say(s)	saying	said	said
send(s)	sending	sent	sent
sit(s)	sitting	sat	sat
speak(s)	speaking	spoke	spoken
take(s)	taking	took	taken
tell(s)	telling	told	told
understand(s)	understanding	understood	understood
win(s)	winning	won	won
write(s)	writing	wrote	written
circle(s)	circling	circled	circled
play(s)	playing	played	played
want(s)	wanting	wanted	wanted
guess(es)	guessing	guessed	guessed

5.1 LISTEN, LOOK, AND READ

Washington is on the one-dollar bill.

Jefferson is on the two-dollar bill.

Lincoln is on the five-dollar bill.

Hamilton is on the ten-dollar bill.

Jackson is on the twenty-dollar bill,

Grant is on the fifty-dollar bill.

Franklin is on the hundred-dollar bill.

5.2 ASK AND ANSWER: PRACTICE IN PAIRS

A. Who's on the _____?

_____ is on the _____.

B. Who's on the _____ and the _____?

_____ is on the _____,

and _____ is on the _____.

5.3 SHOW OR POINT AND ASK

What's this?   That's a _____ dollar bill.

What are these?   Those are a _____ and a
                      _____ dollar bill.

5.4 RITUAL

Excuse me. Can you change a twenty-dollar bill?

What do you need?

I need five ones, a five, and a ten.

Here you are: five ones, a five, and a ten.

Thanks a lot.

Don't mention it.

5.5 ASK AND ANSWER

a	ones
two	five(s)
three	ten(s)
four	twenty/twenties
five	fifty

Excuse me. Can you change

What do you need?

I need _____.

	1	2	3	4	5
ones					
five(s)					
ten(s)					
twent(y/ies)					

Lincoln is on the one-cent coin.

Jefferson is on the five-cent coin.

Roosevelt is on the ten-cent coin.

Washington is on the twenty-five-cent coin.

Kennedy is on the fifty-cent coin.

Sacagawea is on the dollar coin.

COINS

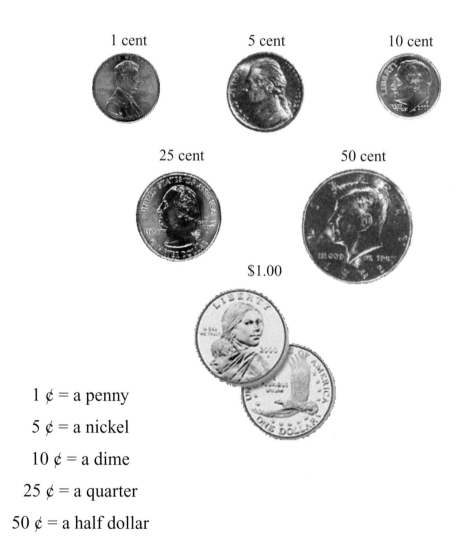

1 cent

5 cent

10 cent

25 cent

50 cent

$1.00

1 ¢ = a penny

5 ¢ = a nickel

10 ¢ = a dime

25 ¢ = a quarter

50 ¢ = a half dollar

5.7 TELL: PRACTICE IN PAIRS

Tell me about the one-cent coin.

_____ is on the one-cent coin.
It's called a _____.
A _____ is worth _____ cent.

Tell me about the five-cent coin.
                  ten-cent coin.
                  twenty-five cent coin.
                  fifty-cent coin.
                  dollar coin.

5.8   ASK AND ANSWER

Do you have change for a dollar?

                                      What do you need?

I need _____.

                                      Let's see. Here you are.
                                      I'm sorry. I don't have _____,
                                      but I can give you _____
                                      Is that okay?

That's good enough. Thanks.

5.9   OPERATION

Pick up a _____ with your right hand.

What did you do?   I picked up a _____.

Put it in your left hand.

What are you doing?   I'm putting it in my left hand.

Now, put it back in your right hand.

What did you do?   _____

Give it to _____.

Stop! What are you going to do?   I'm going to _____.

Go ahead.

Okay. Now tell me what you/he/she did.

How much does a _____ cost?

It costs _____.
Do you want to buy one?

Yes I do. / No, I don't.
No, I can't. I don't have enough money.

dictionary - $6.95

pen - .99

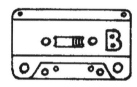

cassette - $2.49

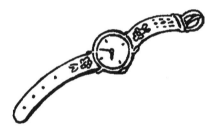

watch - $19.95

pencil - .49

radio - $29.98

TV - $249.50

house - $150,000

(air)plane - $895,000

ASK AND ANSWER

What did you buy?
How much did you spend?

I bought _____.
I spent _____.

5.11 ASK AND ANSWER: WRITE THE PRICE.

A   **Example:**

How much is your coffee?   It's $6.50 a pound,
That's cheap. My coffee is
$7.00 a pound

That's expensive. My coffee is
$6.50 a pound.

> **1 pound (lb.) = .45 kilos**
> **1 kilo = 2.2 pounds**

coffee — /lb.   tea — /lb.   salt — /lb.   sugar — /lb.

rice — /lb.   potatoes — /lb.   tomatoes — /lb.   apples — /lb.

How much is your _____?   It's _____ a pound.
That's cheap/expensive.
My _____ is _____.

5.12 LISTEN AND ANSWER: PRACTICE IN PAIRS

A   Are you hungry?   _____.

Let's go in here;

Get off the street.

Are you thirsty?   _____?

I think you need something to drink.

How do you want it;

Cold or hot?   _____

                    _____.

5.11   ASK AND ANSWER: WRITE THE PRICE.

B   **Example:**

How much is your coffee?   It's $6.50 a pound,
That's cheap. My coffee is
$7.00 a pound

That's expensive. My coffee is
$6.50 a pound.

> **1 pound (lb.) = .45 kilos**
> **1 kilo = 2.2 pounds**

coffee —   /lb.   **tea —   /lb.**   **salt —   /lb.**   **sugar —   /lb.**

rice —   /lb.   **potatoes —   /lb.**   **tomatoes —   /lb.**   **apples —   /lb.**

How much is your _____?   It's _____ a pound.
That's cheap/expensive.
My _____ is _____.

5.12   LISTEN AND ANSWER: PRACTICE IN PAIRS

B   _____?   Yeah, let's eat.

_____;

_____.

_____?   What do you think?

_____

_____.

_____?

_____?   I'll take whatever
                                           they have got.

U. S. Dollar

Euro _____
English Pounds _____
Mexican Peso _____
Australian Dollar _____
Korean Won _____
Swiss Francs _____
Japanese Yen _____
Russian Ruble _____
Canadian Dollar _____
Thai Baht _____
_____ _____
_____ _____

What's a U. S. dollar worth?   It's worth _____ (point) _____
                                 _____ _____s.

How many _____ in a U. S. dollar?   There are _____ in a dollar.

ON THE STREET

Can you change a fifty?

NEW WORDS

change/changed
cost/cost
drink/drank/drunk
eat/ate/eaten
get/got off

have got/had got
mention/mentioned
need/needed
pick/picked up
put/put back

show/showed/shown
spend/spent
stop/stopped
think/thought

(air)plane
apple
bill
cassette
cheap
coffee
coin
cold
dime
dollar
enough
exchange
expensive
half-dollar
hand
hot

hungry
kilo
left (hand)
a lot (of)
nickel
off
penny
picture
point (decimal)
potato
pound
preposition
price
quarter (25¢)
radio
rate

rice
right (hand)
salt
sentence
something
sugar
tea
thirsty
those
today
tomato
watch
whatever
whose
yeah

PRONUNCIATION

/t/	/d/	/id/
asked	agreed	collected
guessed	answered	folded
helped	called	handed
locked	changed	needed
looked	circled	pointed
picked	excused	repeated
practiced	happened	waited
stopped	learned	wanted
watched	listened	
worked	mentioned	
	played	
	saved	

GRAMMAR

HERE	THERE
THIS	THAT
THESE	THOSE

PREPOSITIONS

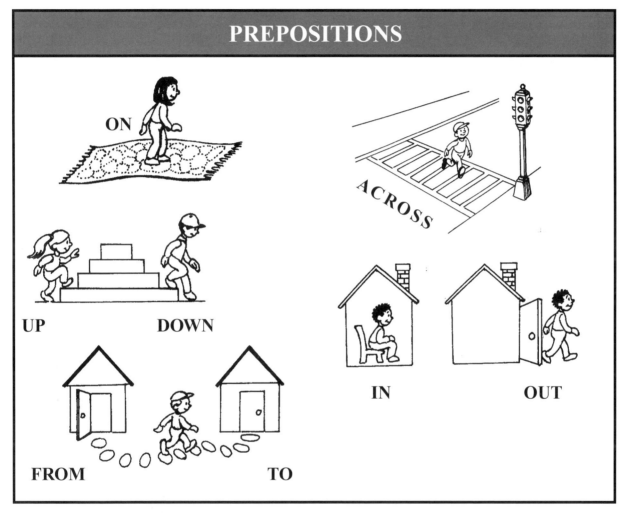

ON

ACROSS

UP   DOWN

IN   OUT

FROM   TO

QUESTION WORDS

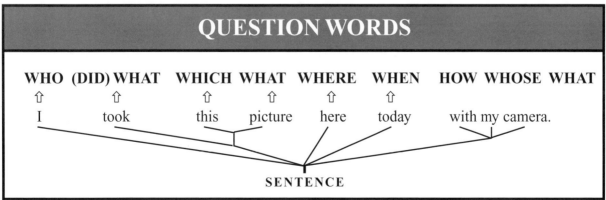

WHO (DID) WHAT   WHICH WHAT   WHERE   WHEN   HOW WHOSE WHAT

I   took   this picture   here   today   with my camera.

SENTENCE

6.1 LISTEN, READ, AND SAY THE TIME

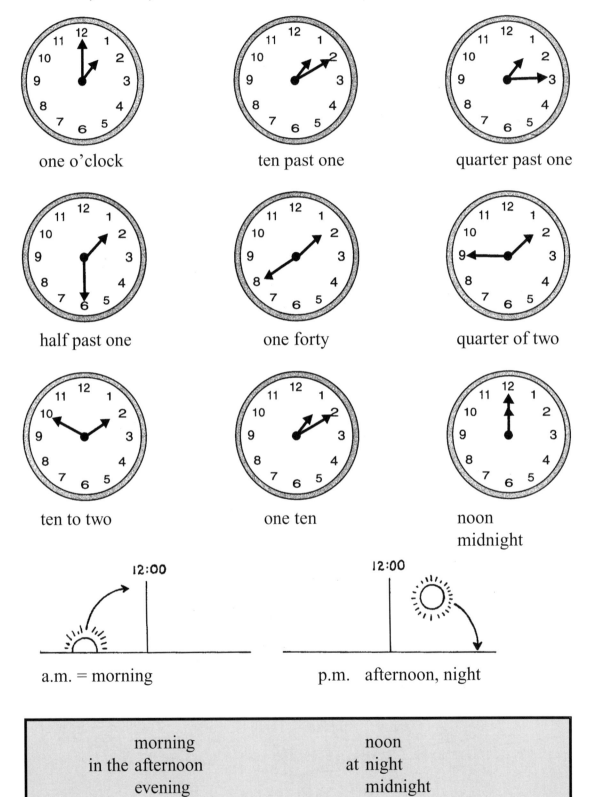

one o'clock

ten past one

quarter past one

half past one

one forty

quarter of two

ten to two

one ten

noon
midnight

12:00

a.m. = morning

12:00

p.m.   afternoon, night

morning	noon
in the afternoon	at night
evening	midnight

A

Do you have the time?   Yes. It's _____.
Thank you.

                               Let's see. We have a class at _____.

I think we'll be late/on time/early.

B

Calendar
for the month of
January

WEEKDAYS					WEEKEND	
MONDAY	TUESDAY	WEDNESDAY	THURSDAY	FRIDAY	SATURDAY	SUNDAY
1	2	3	4	5	6	7
8	9	10	11	12	13	14
15	16	17	18	19	20	21
22	23	24	25	26	27	28
29	30	31				

6.3 POINT, ASK, AND ANSWER

What day is today?	It's _____.
What's tomorrow?	It's _____.
What's the day after tomorrow?	It's _____.
What was yesterday?	It was _____.
What was the day before yesterday?	It was _____.

6.4 POINT, ASK, AND ANSWER

What's today's date?   It's the _____.

1st = first	4th = fourth	7th = seventh	10th = tenth	20th = twentieth
2nd = second	5th = fifth	8th = eighth	11th = eleventh	21st = twenty first
3rd = third	6th = sixth	9th = ninth	12th = twelfth	30th = thirtieth

6.5 POINT, ASK, AND ANSWER

What's today?   It's _____day, the _____ of January.

6.6 ASK AND ANSWER: PRACTICE IN PAIRS

What's on TV tonight?

How about _____ on channel _____
at _____ o'clock?

Maybe, but how about _____?

I think it's about/a _____.
               or
I don't know what it's about.

I don't know. Let's take a look.

That looks interesting, but how
about _____?

What's it about?

TV Tonight

	8:00	9:00	10:00
CH 2	Airplanes	It's Your Birthday	Dollars and Cents
CH 3	A Month of Sundays	Get Rich!	English Interplay
CH 4	What's the Price?	The Long Wait	Spell It Right!
CH 5	Your Cats and Dogs	Winners and Losers	Ten Is Enough
CH 6	All About Eve	The Big Apple	My Friend Friday
CH 7	At Home with Edna	Dog Day Afternoon	The Midnight Hour
CH 8	Wait a Minute!	Another Year	Holiday in Mexico
CH 9	Today's Schedule	April in Paris	Beth and Bess

6.7 ASK AND ANSWER: PRACTICE IN PAIRS

So, at _____ we'll watch _____.

And at _____ we'll watch _____.

And at _____ we'll
watch _____.

The Year and the Holidays

January	**February**	**March**
New Year's Day	Presidents' Day	
Martin Luther King, Jr. Day		

April	**May**	**June**
	Memorial Day	

July	**August**	**September**
Independence Day		Labor Day

October	**November**	**December**
Columbus Day	Veterans Day	Christmas
	Thanksgiving	

Other days: Valentine's Day: February 14
Halloween: October 31
Mother's Day: 2nd Sunday in May
Father's Day: 3rd Sunday in June

6.9   **ASK AND ANSWER**

When is _____(Holiday)?   It's in _____(month).

6.10 ASK AND ANSWER WITH THIS YEAR'S CALENDAR

This year, when is _____ (Holiday)?

This year, _____ (Holiday) is
on _____ (day) the _____
of _____ (month).

6.11 ASK AND ANSWER

When is _____ (Holiday)?   It's in the _____.

6.12 PRACTICE

How many seconds in a minute?
There are always sixty in it.
How many minutes in an hour?
Always sixty in one hour.

Twenty-four hours is a day.
Each week has seven days.
And twelve are the months in a year.
But February's a little queer.

Thirty days has September,
April, June and November.
All the rest have thirty-one,
But February's a special one.

Twenty-eight most of the time,
But once in four, it's twenty-nine.

6.13 ASK YOUR CLASSMATES

When is your birthday?

It's on _____.

So, it's on the _____.

Classmates' Birthdays

CLASSMATE	BIRTHDAY
_____	_____
_____	_____
_____	_____
_____	_____
_____	_____
_____	_____
_____	_____
_____	_____

6.14 PRACTICE IN PAIRS

What's the matter?	Nothing at all.
What's the problem?	No problem at all.
Can I help?	There's nothing wrong.
Are you sure?	As the day is long.
Are you okay?	Can't you see?
What can I do?	Don't bother me.
Then I will go.	Have a nice day..
Okay, so long.	And by the way . . .
Yes, go on.	Yesterday?
Yesterday?	Somebody's birthday?

6.15 ASK YOUR CLASSMATES

Tomorrow I've (I have) got to _____, and next week _____.

What have you got to do?

PERSON	TOMORROW	NEXT WEEK
_____	_____	_____
_____	_____	_____
_____	_____	_____
_____	_____	_____
_____	_____	_____
_____	_____	_____
_____	_____	_____
_____	_____	_____
_____	_____	_____

What has _____ got to do?   _____'s got to _____.

6.16 PRACTICE AND REVIEW

Open your book.
What are you going to do?   I'm going to open my book.
Turn to page _____. (8,20,30,40,50)
What did you do?   I turned to page _____.
Now look at the words on page _____.
Find three words that you don't know.
Write them here.
_____
_____
_____

Now let's write six words on the board.

NEW WORDS

Verbs

bother	have got to	open	turn

Others

after	February	midnight	past	that
always	Friday	Monday	problem	third
April	holiday	month	queer	Thursday
August	hour	most	(the) rest	tomorrow
before	interesting	next	Saturday	tonight
birthday	January	night	season	Tuesday
calendar	July	noon	second	Wednesday
(o') clock	June	nothing	second (2nd)	week
date	a little	November	September	weekday
December	March	October	so long	weekend
each	matter	once	special	winter
early	May	on time	summer	year
fall	maybe	other	Sunday	

ON THE STREET

Do you have the right time?

GRAMMAR

NOUN + S	NOUN + ø
I bought some (3-6) books. a few (2-3) a lot of (10) seven (7)	a little (1 lb.) I bought some (2-4 lb.) sugar.* a lot of (10 lb.) seven pounds of
I didn't buy any (0) books. many (2-3)	I didn't buy any (0) sugar.* much (2-3 lb.)

* sugar, salt, coffee, tea, rice, paper, money, time, homework

+	−	?

HAVE

You have some	You don't have any	Do you have any
She has some	She doesn't have any	Does she have any

HAVE TO

You have to have	You don't have to have	Do you have to have
She has to have	She doesn't have to have	Does she have to have

HAVE GOT TO

You have got to have	You haven't got to have	Have you got to have
She has got to have	She hasn't got to have	Has she got to have

---

I know the answer.
She knows the answer.

I may know the answer.
She may know the answer.

I want to know the answer.
She wants to know the answer.

I think (that) I know the answer.
She thinks (that) she knows the answer.

What **is it** about?
I know what **it is** about.
I don't know what **it is** about.
Do you know what **it is** about?

What **does she know**?
I know what **she knows**.
I don't know what **she knows**.
Do you know what **she knows**?

7.1 READ AND STUDY EDNA'S FAMILY.

EDNA'S FAMILY

(Edna and her relatives)

Betsy	Peter	Arthur	Nell
Green	Green	Smith	Smith
1919	1915-1990	1914	1915-1988

David	Mary	Fred	Nancy (Smith)
Green	Green-Smith	Smith	Brown
1940	1936	1935	1933-1999

Wendy	Edna ————	Ed	Jim
Smith	Worth	Worth	Smith
1958	1956	1949	1956-1974

Ted	Beth
Worth	Worth
1980	1978

My name is Edna. I am married. My spouse is Ed Worth. He is my husband. I am his spouse. I am his wife. We have two children. My son is Ted. He is single. My daughter is Beth. She also is single. I had one brother. He was Jim Smith. He was my twin brother. We were born in 1956. He died several years ago in 1974. I have one sister. She is Wendy Smith. Our mother and father are alive. They were married in 1955. Nancy is my aunt. David is my uncle. My mother's mother is my grandmother. She is alive. My mother's father is my grandfather. He is dead. My husband's mother, my mother in-law, is also dead.

ASK AND ANSWER THESE QUESTIONS WITH A PARTNER

Who is _____ _____?

He/She is Edna's _____.

Who is Edna's _____.

He/She is _____ _____.

7.2   THIS IS MY FAMILY

ME

7.3   DESCRIBE YOUR FAMILY

My name is _____. My _____'s name is

_____   _____.

EDNA'S FAMILY'S BIRTHDAYS

Edna: November 23, 1956   Arthur: July 13, 1914

Ed: February 21, 1949   Nell: January 3, 1915

Beth: August 4, 1978   Mary: June 22, 1936

Ted: March 25, 1980   Betsy: October 2, 1919

Wendy: May 30, 1958   Fred: September 17, 1935

Jim: November 23, 1956   Peter: December 5, 1915

David: February 29, 1940   Nancy: April 1, 1933

Nell Smith died on December 30, 1988
Peter Green died on March 19, 1990
Jim Smith died on October 10, 1974
Nancy Brown died on January 21, 1999

7.4   ASK AND ANSWER ABOUT EDNA'S FAMILY

When is _____'s birthday?

_____'s birthday is on _____.

When was _____ born?

_____ was born on _____.

How old is _____?

_____ is _____years old.
_____ is dead. He/She died _____
years ago.

MY FAMILY'S BIRTHDAYS

_____   _____

_____   _____

_____   _____

_____   _____

_____   _____

_____   _____

FAMOUS PEOPLE

Genghis Khan 1162-1227
Marco Polo 1254-1324
Dante Alighieri 1265-1321
Joan of Arc   1412-1431
Leonardo da Vinci 1452-1519
Queen Elizabeth I 1558-1603
William Shakespeare 1564-1616
George Washington 1732-1799
Napoleon Bonaparte 1769-1821
Ludwig van Beethoven 1770-1827
Simon Bolivar 1783-1830
Sacagawea 1788-1812
Benito Juarez 1806-1872
Mahatma Gandhi 1869-1948
Winston Churchill 1874-1965

Syngman Rhee 1875-1965
Kemal Ataturk 1881-1938
John F. Kennedy 1917-1963
Anwar al-Sadat 1918-1981
Nelson Mandela 1918-
Evita 1919-1952
Pierre Trudeau 1919-2000
Queen Elizabeth II 1926-
Martin Luther King, Jr. 1929-1968
Mikhail Gorbachev 1931-
Dalai Lama 1935-
King Hussein 1935-1999
Kofi Annan   1938-
John Lennon 1940-1980
Princess Diana 1961-1997

7.5   MATCH THESE FAMOUS PEOPLE WITH THE COUNTRIES

Germany	India	Egypt	France
Turkey	Italy	Argentina	America
Mongolia	Russia	Jordan	South Africa
Ghana	England	Mexico	Tibet
Korea	/Great Britain	Canada	Venezuela

_____ is/was from _____.

He/She is/was a(n) _____.

7.6   ASK AND ANSWER
WHERE ARE YOU AND YOUR CLASSMATES FROM?

_____   _____
_____   _____
_____   _____
_____   _____
_____   _____
_____   _____

7.7   LISTEN, READ AND SAY THE ADDRESSES

(See p. 71 for abbreviations)

This is Edna's address:
Mrs. Edna Worth
197 Center St.
Middle Corners, VT 05001

This is Edna's parents' address:
Mr. and Mrs. Fred Smith
Apt. 21-B, 300 Northern Blvd.
E. Centerville, NM 87100

This is Edna's son's address:
Mr. Ted Worth
P.O. Box 1330
W. Bridgewater, ME 04822

This is Edna's sister's address:
Ms. Wendy Smith
33 Eastern Ave.
Northfield, Ontario N2J 3Z9

Edna's daughter's address:
Miss Beth Worth
2250 Upper Airport Rd.
S. Bridgeport, WV 26330

Edna's friend
Annie Suquet
3 Riverside Rd.
River City, NB E2L 5L4

Edna's friend
Elise Carlson
17 Lower Main Street
Watertown, SD 57201

Edna's friend
Judy Beaudoin
281 Middle Street
Greenville, NC 27834

7.8   ASK AND ANSWER

Who lives in _____(State/Province)_____?   _____ does.

Where does _____ live, in _(State/Province)_?   In ___(City)___.

What is _____'s address and zip/postal code?   It's _____.

Is _____ married or unmarried/single?

_____ is _____.

I don't know if _____ is _____ or _____.

VT Vermont	**NM** New Mexico	**NC** North Carolina
ME Maine	**WV** West Virginia	**SD** South Dakota
	NB New Brunswick	

Mr. = married or unmarried man	**Mrs.** = married woman
Ms = married or unmarried woman	**Miss** = unmarried woman

7.9 WRITE YOUR ADDRESS HERE:

```



```

7.10 ASK YOUR CLASSMATES FOR THEIR ADDRESSES. WRITE THEM HERE:

7.11 READ, PRACTICE, AND TELL YOUR PARTNER

I want to send a letter to a friend. What do I have to do?

First, you have to write the address in the center of the envelope.

You write the person's name on the top line.

Then you write the street or the post office box on the middle line.

Next, the city, state/province and zip code on the bottom line.

Then you have to write your return address in the upper left-hand corner.

  Actually, you don't have to. You can write it on the back of the envelope.

Then you put the stamp in the upper right-hand corner.

Finally, you have to put the letter in the envelope and seal it.

7.12   SAY THESE PHONE NUMBERS

EXAMPLE:

Smith, Mary and Fred	603 - 926-3405	Area code six oh three nine two six three four oh five

Worth, Edna and Ed	802-257-3413	Carlson, Elise	605-787-1265
Worth, Beth	304-796-0145	Beaudoin, Judy	252-590-4591
Worth, Ted	207-340-7779	Suquet, Annie	505-456-9915
Smith, Wendy	519-994-7067	Smith, Fred	506-433-8019
Green, Betsy	201-770-3498	Burrows, Arthur	800-257-5117
Smith, Arthur	602-147-5048	Bush, George W.	202-456-7041

7.13   HOW TO USE A PHONE

Pick up the phone. . . . . .What did you do?, etc.
Listen for the dial tone.
Dial the number.
Wait for an answer.
When someone answers, begin talking.
Talk.
Say goodbye.
Hang up.

ON THE STREET

May I use the phone?

7.14 READ AND THEN TELL YOUR PARTNER
HOW TO USE DIRECTORY ASSISTANCE.

USE "IF" TEN TIMES.

ACPC
DIRECTORY ASSISTANCE

Our operators have millions of numbers. Please call when you need a number.
We can help.

HOW TO DIAL DIRECTORY ASSISTANCE

For numbers in your area code 411

For numbers anywhere in North America 411

For toll-free numbers 411

For coin telephones . . . . See instructions on the phone

DIRECTORY ASSISTANCE COSTS

If your call is inside your own area code, no charge for the first three calls each month.
After that, each call costs 64 cents.

If you dial O for an operator, the call costs 92 cents.

Outside your own area code, if you call directory assistance, the call costs 95 cents.

Let us help you.

AMERICAN AND CANADIAN PHONE COMPANY
YOUR PHONE COMPANY FROM THE ATLANTIC TO THE PACIFIC

NEW WORDS

VERBS

describe	live	study
dial	match	talk
die	return	use
hang up	seal	

NOUNS

abbreviation	dial tone	Mrs.
address	directory	Ms.
adjective	envelope	noun
airport	family	operator
assistance	father	parent
avenue	grandfather	partner
aunt	grandmother	post office
boulevard	husband	relative
box	instruction	road
brother	letter	sister
center	life/lives	someone
charge	line	son
city	Miss	spouse
company	Mister	twin
corner	mother	uncle
daughter	mother-in-law	wife

ADJECTIVES

alive	(un)married	south(ern)
bottom	middle	toll-free
dead	north(ern)	top
east(ern)	old	upper
famous	several	west(ern)
lower	single	

OTHERS

actually	born	inside
ago	finally	outside
also	if	own
anywhere		

GRAMMAR

BE: PRESENT, PAST, AND PRESENT PERFECT

I **am** single now.
I **was** single several years ago.
I **have been** single for several years.

She **is** single now.
She **was** single several years ago.
She **has been** single for several years.

You/We/They **are** single now.
You/We/They **were** single several years ago.
You/We/They **have been** single for several years.

VERB	NOUNS
direct	directory
	direction
	director
operate	operation
	operator
instruct	instruction
	instructor
collect	collection
	collector
correct	correction
describe	description
repeat	repetition

ABBREVIATIONS

a.m.	morning	**Jr.**	Junior	**N.**	North	**lb.**	pound
p.m.	afternoon	**Sr.**	Senior	**S.**	South	**oz.**	ounce
b.	born	**ex.**	example	**E.**	East	**gr.**	gram
d.	died	**etc.**	etcetera	**W.**	West	**kg.**	kilogram
Mr.	Mister	**p.**	page	**St.**	Street		
Mrs.	/misiz/	**P.O.**	post office	**Ave.**	Avenue		
Ms	/miz/	**tel.**	telephone	**Rd.**	Road		
		no.	number	**Blvd.**	Boulevard		

LESSON 8

A BLOCK IN RIVER CITY

This is a block in downtown River City.

The River City Hotel is in the middle of the block.

It is between a drugstore and a bank.

The drug store is next to City Hall.

There are two people in front of the hotel.

There is a taxi in front of the hotel.

There are three cars and a truck on Main Street

There are two people and a dog in front of City Hall.

There are two people at the bus stop on the corner of Main and Valley Streets.

There is a bus at the bus stop.

There is nobody in front of the bank.

There is no one in front of the drug store.

There is an apartment building behind the bank.

There is a sign on top of Downtown Apartments.

There is an office building beside the apartment building and in back of the hotel.

8.2   ASK AND ANSWER

How many _____(s) are _____ the _____?

There is/are _____.

Where is/are the _____?

It is/they are _____.

8.3   MAKE A CITY BLOCK. SHOW AND DESCRIBE IT.

A MAP OF RIVER CITY

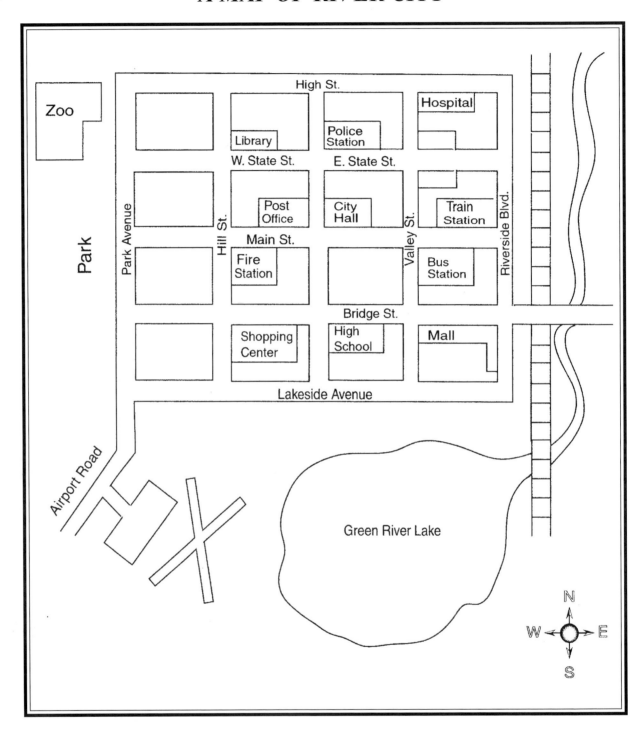

8.4 GIVE INSTRUCTIONS TO YOUR PARTNER

You are at the corner of _____ and _____.

You want to go to _____.

8.5   NOW ASK FOR AND GIVE DIRECTIONS

Excuse me, can you tell me how to get to _____?

Well, let's see. Walk E/N/S/W along _____.

Turn left/right at _____.

Continue until _____.

Is it very far?

No, it's quite near.

It's only _____block(s) from here.

Would you repeat those directions?

Sure. _____.

So, I _____.

That's right.

Thanks a lot for your help.

No problem.

8.6   LISTEN

Let's take a tour by car around River City. This is what we will do. We will start at the train station. We will drive south on Riverside. We will pass the mall on our right. We will turn right on Lakeside. We will go past the lake. When we come to Airport Road, we will turn right on Park Avenue. We will drive past the park and finish our tour at the zoo.

DESCRIBE WHAT YOU'RE DOING AS YOU TAKE YOUR TOUR

Ex: We are starting at the train station. We are going south on Riverside, etc., etc.

TELL WHAT YOU DID ON YOUR TOUR

Ex: We started at the train station. We went south on Riverside, etc.,etc.

8.7   NOW GIVE YOUR PARTNER A DIFFERENT TOUR

```
A                          E                          C




















D                          F                          B
```

Draw a line from A to B.

What are you going to do?
What are you doing?
What have you done?
What did you do?

This line will be Cross Street.
Write Cross Street along the line.

Now draw a line from E to F.
This will be Center Street.

Next, draw a line from A to C.
Name this street.

Draw a line from D to E.
Draw a line from A to D.
Name these streets.

8.9   NOW TAKE TURNS

Put an X on _____ street. This will be a/the _____.

AT THE MALL

8.10 READ AND STUDY

Someone is coming in the entrance.

No one is going out the exit.

Someone is getting into an elevator.

Someone is getting out of the other elevator.

No one is going up the stairs.

Someone is coming down the stairs.

Someone is walking toward the exit.

Someone else is walking away from the exit.

8.11 ASK AND ANSWER

Is anyone coming in the entrance?

Is anyone _____?

Yes, someone is coming in the entrance.

Yes/No, _____.

What's this thing/stuff?   I think it's _____.
Yeah, I think so too.
          or
No, I don't think so. I think
it's _____.

8.13　FIND OUT WHAT EVERYONE HAS AND WHAT NO ONE HAS

A.　_____, I think you have
　　a/some _____?

　　　　　　　　　　　　　　　　　　No, you're wrong, I don't.
　　　　　　　　　　　　　　　　　　You're right, I do.

　　Aha! So someone has a/some _____.

B.　I think I know what everyone has and what no one has.

　　It looks like a few people people have _____,
　　but everyone has _____ and
　　no one has _____.

8.14　PRATICE IN PAIRS

Where can you get anything that you want?　　At Mike and Andy's Restaurant.
Can you get breakfast?　　　　　　　　　　Yes, you can.
Can you get lunch?　　　　　　　　　　　　Sure, you can.
Can you get dinner?　　　　　　　　　　　Of course you can.
You can get anything you want.　　　　　　　At Mike and Andy's Restaurant.

ON THE STREET

Excuse me, I'm lost. Can you tell me where 99 Main is?

NEW WORDS

VERBS

come/came/came
continue
draw/drew/drawn
drive/drove/driven
find/found out

finish
get/got into
get/got out of
get/got to

look like
pass
start
walk

NOUNS

bank
block
breakfast
bridge
building
bus
bus stop
dinner
direction
drug store
elevator
entrance
exit

fire station
hall
high school
hospital
hotel
lake
library
mall
office
park
police station
restaurant
review

river
shopping center
sign
stairs
stuff
taxi
thing
tour
train station
truck
turn
valley
zoo

PREPOSITIONS

along
around
away from
behind
beside

between
by
in back of
in front of

next to
on top of
past
toward

OTHERS

a few
anyone
anything
as
downtown
else

everyone
far
lost
near
nobody
no one

of course
only
there is/are
until
well

GRAMMAR

+	−	?
There is	There isn't	Is there
There are	There aren't	Are there

PREPOSITIONS

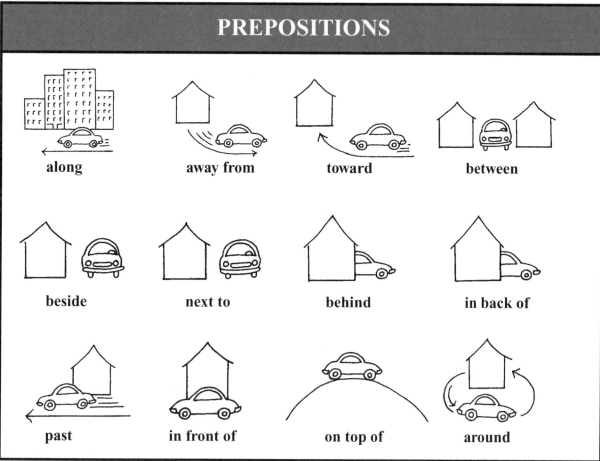

along

away from

toward

between

beside

next to

behind

in back of

past

in front of

on top of

around

a / the

This is **a** hotel.
The hotel is beside **a** bank.
The bank is beside **a** restaurant.
The restaurant is near **a** bus stop.
There is **a** bus at **the** bus stop.
The bus stop is on ø Valley Street.

ø / some / the

I want to buy ø coffee.
I bought **some** coffee.
The coffee was very good.
I want to buy ø apples.
I bought **some** apples.
The apples were very good.

LESSON 9

9.1 POINT, ASK, AND IDENTIFY

Do you remember who this is?

I think it's _____.

police officer	_____	A. works in a hospital
civil engineer	_____	B. drives buses
teller	_____	C. works in a zoo
waiter	_____	D. flies (air)planes
cashier	_____	E. builds bridges
nurse	_A_	F. works in a store
bus driver	_____	G. works in a law office
truck driver	_____	H. works in a toy store
doctor	_____	I. works in a bank
pilot	_____	J. works in a post office
accountant	_____	K. drives trucks
cook	_____	L. works in a hospital
zoo keeper	_____	M. works in a restaurant
postal clerk	_____	N. works in a police station
toy store clerk	_____	O. works in an office
lawyer	_____	P. works in a restaurant

What does a(n)_____ do?

A(n) _____ _____ _____.

9.3   WRITE AND GIVE THEM A JOB

A

p_____ o_____

c_____

b_____ d_____

w_____

t_____ s_____ c_____

a_____

c_____

l_____

9.4   ASK AND ANSWER

What's _____'s job?   He/She 's a(n) _____.

Where does he/she work?   He/She works _____.
            or
What does a(n) do?   He/She _____ _____s.

B

n_____

c_____ e_____

z_____ k_____

p_____

t _____

p_____ c_____

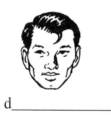

d_____

t_____ d_____

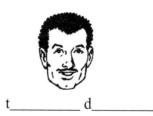

t_____ d_____

9.4   ASK AND ANSWER

What's _____'s job?   He/She 's a(n) _____.

Where does he/she work?   He/She works _____.
      or
What does a(n) do?   He/She _____ _____s.

9.5   ASK AND ANSWER

(Jill is working on a bridge. Where is everyone else working?)

Where is _____ working?

He/She is working in _____.

How long has _____ been
a(n) _____?

He/She's been a(n) _____
for _____.

So, he/she has been working
as a(n) _____ for _____.

That's right.

9.6   INTRODUCE ONE PERSON TO ANOTHER

_____x_____, I'd like to introduce _____y_____.

_____x_____, this is _____y_____.

_____y_____, this is _____x_____.

How do you do _____y_____?

Nice to meet you,_____x_____.

_____y_____ is my friend. He/She is a(n) _____.

Oh, really? That's nice.
That's interesting.
Where do you work?
How long have you been _____?

9.7   ASK AND ANSWER

What does _____ like to do after work?

_____ likes to _____.

watch TV	go for a walk	listen to music
go to the library	relax at home	read the paper
read a book	surf the net	go to a bar
jog in the park	check his/her email	go to the gym
walk the dog	play with his/her children	play video games
	watch videos	

Eve   _____

Jill   _____

Gus   _____

Max   _____

Jon   _____

Joe   _____

Bert   _____

Ruth   _____

Jeff   _____

Mike   _____

Chuck   _____

Paul   _____

Howie   _____

Janie   _____

Zoey   _____

Brooke _____

9.8   ASK AND ANSWER

Why does _____ like to _____?   Because it's _____.

fun	exciting	relaxing	interesting
enjoyable	informative	necessary	restful

9.9 INTERVIEW YOUR CLASSMATES

NAME	JOB	AFTER WORK

9.10 WRITE AND TELL ABOUT YOURSELF AND YOUR FAMILY

HELP WANTED

STORE CLERK – Roy's Toys. 30 hrs/wk. Apply in person $9.00/hr. Call 254-3413	**BANK TELLER** – RiverCitiBank 40 hrs./wk. Starts at $9.00/hr. Call 257-1310. Ask for Mr. Rein
WAITERS – Mike and Andy's. Lunch and Dinner. Call Mike at 257-7791.	**TAXICAB DRIVER** – CITY CAB CO. Nights. $11.00/hr. Interview necessary. Call 254-TAXI
NURSE – River City Hospital. 8 a.m. - 4 p.m. Call for an interview. 254-7038	**TRUCK DRIVER** – CHUCK'S TRUCKING. Experience necessary. Good money. 257- 7507.
COOK – McBurgers. Experience not necessary. Call Carlos at 258-3300. Starting at $11.50.	**HOUSEKEEPER** – River City Hotel. Starts at $9.50. Call 254-3000
CASHIER – PRM Drug Store. Begin immediately. Call Pat at 257-5461.	**BOOKKEEPER** – River City College, Accounting Dept. Ask for Steve at 257-7751.

9.11   APPLY FOR A JOB

I would like to apply for the job
at _____.
Please tell me about it.

It's _____.

Thank you.

Now tell me why you want this job.

9.12   WHAT WILL YOU DO?

First, I will call for information.
I will get an application.
I will fill it out.
I will ask for an interview.
I will go for the interview.
I will introduce myself.
I will explain why I want the job.

What will you do next?

NEW WORDS

VERBS

apply	fill out	introduce	relax
build/built/built	fly/flew/flown	jog	remember
check	identify	like	surf
drive/drove/driven	interview	meet/met	would like to
explain			

NOUNS

accountant	dept./department	information	postal clerk
bar	doctor	law(yer)	store
bookkeeper	driver	music	teller
cab	email	(inter)net	toy
cashier	experience	nurse	video
clerk	gym	(news)paper	waiter
cook	housekeeper	pilot	zoo keeper

OTHERS

because	fun	necessary	-self
enjoyable	immediately	really	why
exciting	in person	restful	

ON THE STREET

Does this bus go to the zoo?

GRAMMAR

<table>
<tr><td>**+**</td><td>**–**</td><td>**?**</td></tr>
<tr>
<td>You have been working.
She has been working.</td>
<td>You have not been working.
She has not been working.</td>
<td>Have you been working?
Has she been working?</td>
</tr>
</table>

WH ?

Where have you been working?
Where has she been working?

(WOULD) LIKE

	I	**like**	cars to drive driving
	I	**would like**	a new car
	I	**would like to**	drive

I **would** = I'd

<table>
<tr><td>**+**</td><td>**–**</td><td>**?**</td></tr>
<tr>
<td>you will go
you'll go</td>
<td>you will not go
you won't go</td>
<td>will you go
will you go</td>
</tr>
</table>

<u>who</u>   <u>what</u>   <u>where</u>   <u>when</u>   <u>why</u>   <u>who</u>   <u>what</u>   <u>what</u>
I will drive to Boston tomorrow because I don't like flying.

LESSON 10

10.1 LISTEN, WATCH AND DRAW: LET'S MAKE A FACE

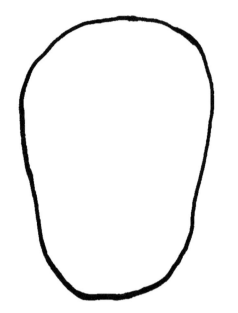

hair

eyes

eyebrows

ear

nose

mouth

tooth/teeth

lips

10.2 ASK AND ANSWER

Am I touching my _____?

Yes, you are.
No you aren't. You're touching your
_____.

10.3 ASK YOUR CLASSMATES

Person	Hair Color	Eye Color
_____	_____	_____
_____	_____	_____
_____	_____	_____
_____	_____	_____
_____	_____	_____
_____	_____	_____
_____	_____	_____

1. head

2. _____

3. shoulder

4. _____

5. elbow

6. _____

7. hand

8. _____

9. thumb

10. _____

11. stomach

12. _____

13. hips

14. _____

15. knee

16. _____

17. foot

18. _____

REX WRECKER

What's number _____?

It's the _____(s).

1. _____

2. neck

3. _____

4. arm

5. _____

6. wrist

7. _____

8. fingers

9. _____

10. chest

11. _____

12. waist

13. _____

14. leg

15. _____

16. ankle

17. _____

18. toes

VENUS VAMPIRA

What's number _____?

It's the _____(s).

10.5 SAY PLEASE GAME

Please touch your _____.

                    I'm touching my _____.

Touch your _____.

                    Say please.

Please touch your _____.

                    I'm touching my _____.

10.6 FOLLOW THE DIRECTIONS: GYM CLASS

Turn your head to the left.	I'm turning my head to the left.
Turn your head to the right.	I'm turning my head to the right.
Shake your shoulders left and right.	I'm shaking my shoulders left and right.
Now bend your left arm.	I am bending my left arm.
Now bend your right arm.	I am bending my right arm.
Now twist your wrist.	Now I'm twisting my wrist.
Now shake your head.	Now I'm shaking my head.
Now twist your hips.	Now I'm twisting my hips.
Bend down at the waist.	I'm bending down at the waist.
Now touch your toes.	Now I'm touching my toes.
Now straighten up.	Now I'm straightening up.
Let's do it all again.	Do it again? I've had enough!

10.7   ASK AND ANSWER

How much do you weigh?

I weigh about _____ pounds.

CLASSMATE	WEIGHT
_____	_____
_____	_____
_____	_____
_____	_____
_____	_____
_____	_____
_____	_____
_____	_____
_____	_____
_____	_____
_____	_____
_____	_____

10.8   TELL ABOUT YOUR CLASSMATES

_____'s weight is _____.

_____ weighs more/less than _____.

_____ and _____ weigh about the same.

10.9   ASK AND ANSWER

How tall are you?

I am _____ feet, _____ inches tall.

How old are you?

I am _____ years old.

CLASSMATE	HEIGHT	AGE
_____	_____	_____
_____	_____	_____
_____	_____	_____
_____	_____	_____
_____	_____	_____
_____	_____	_____
_____	_____	_____
_____	_____	_____
_____	_____	_____

10.10   TELL ABOUT YOUR CLASSMATES

LINE UP BY HEIGHT

_____ is taller/shorter than _____.

_____ is the tallest/shortest.

LINE UP BY AGE

_____ is younger/older than _____.

_____ is the youngest/oldest.

10.11   DESCRIBE THESE PEOPLE

USE THESE WORDS:

tall	young	big
short	old	small

definitely not clearly not	possibly	probably	clearly definitely
0%		50%	100%

10.12   ASK AND ANSWER: PRACTICE IN PAIRS

You look sleepy. Are you tired?

No, not me. I'm really wired.

You seem sick. Are you well?

I feel fine. I'm really swell.

You look bored. Is that true?

That's because I'm listening to you.

What do you do every day?

Relax for a while   _____

Get dressed   _____

Come back home   _____

Wash my face   _____

Go to bed   _____

Get up   _____

Sleep all night   _____

Brush my teeth   _____

Work all day   _____

Take a shower   _____

Have breakfast   _____

Go to work   _____

10.14   TELL ▓▓▓▓▓▓▓▓▓▓▓▓▓▓▓▓▓▓▓▓▓▓▓▓▓▓

How long or what time do you do these things?

How often do you do them?

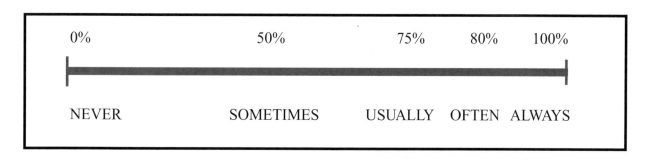

NEVER   SOMETIMES   USUALLY   OFTEN   ALWAYS

A Short Play in Three Acts

ACT ONE

A _____ : I've been looking everywhere for you. Where have you been?
B _____ : Nowhere.
A _____ : What have you been doing?
B _____ : Nothing.
A _____ : Nowhere? Nothing?
B _____ : Well, I just went in the bookstore for a few minutes.
A _____ : Anyway, Let's go somewhere and get something to eat.
B _____ : Where do you want to go?
A _____ : Oh, anywhere.
B _____ : Let's go to McBurger's.
A _____ : Nobody goes there anymore. Everybody goes to Mike and Andy's these days.
B _____ : Okay. I don't want to be a nobody.

ACT TWO

A _____ : Here we are. Will you have anything to drink?
B _____ : I don't think so. Let's find someone to wait on us.
A _____ : By the way, somebody told me that Andy's eggplant special is something else. Simply the best!
B _____ : I don't see any waiters anywhere.
A _____ : You're right. I don't see anyone, either.
B _____ : Look! Here comes Mike.
C _____ : Hi. Is everything okay?
B _____ : Uh, not really. No one is waiting on us.
C _____ : Oh, I'm really sorry about that. Everyone is really busy, but I'll take your order.
A _____ : Great! So what's good?
C _____ : Everything, of course, but Andy's eggplant is really super.
B _____ : Eggplant soup?
C _____ : No. I said super — better than good!
A _____ : Well, I'll try anything. The eggplant special for me.
B _____ : I'll have the soup and sandwich special.

ACT THREE

B _____ : You said everybody comes here. Do you see anybody we know?
A _____ : Not really. I think they're all tourists. Ah, here comes Mike with our order.
C _____ : Here you are. Enjoy!
A _____ : Thanks, Mike.
C _____ : Andy says hello. He'd love to see you, but he's really busy.
A _____ : You're always busy here. Every time I come there's a crowd.

C _____ : Yeah. It's usually crowded. Our business isn't bad nowadays.
A _____ : It looks like your business is getting better and better.
B _____ : And you're probably getting richer and richer.
C _____ : Well, we're certainly busier and busier. See you later.

(Exit Mike)

B _____ : Their business may be getting better and better, but the service is getting worse and worse. So, how's the eggplant special?
A _____ : Excellent. I've never had better. How's the soup?
B _____ : It's okay. I've had worse.
A _____ : Here's Mike again.
C _____ : Are you still working on it?
B _____ : Working? No, I'm still eating.
C _____ : Of course. I'll come back.

(Exit Mike)

B _____ : Eating is working?
A _____ : Oh, everybody says that.
B _____ : Well, I'm not going to "work" here again.
A _____ : You should have had the eggplant.
B _____ : Oh yeah? I think we should have gone somewhere else.

ON THE STREET

Is anybody here?

NEW WORDS

VERBS

bend/bent/bent
brush
come/came back
feel/felt
follow

get/got dressed
get/got up
line up
look (seem)
look for

love
seem
shake/shook/shaken
sleep/slept
straighten

touch
try
wait on
wash
weigh

NOUNS

age
ankle
arm
bed
business
chest
crowd
ear
elbow
eye

eyebrow
face
finger
foot/feet
hair
head
height
hip
inch
knee

leg
lip
mouth
neck
nose
order
sandwich
service
shoulder
shower

soup
stomach
thumb
toe
tooth/teeth
tourist
waist
weight
(a) while
wrist

ADJECTIVES

about
better/best
bored
busy
excellent

less
more
rich
same
sick

short
sleepy
small
super
swell

tall
true
wired
worse
young

ADVERBS

anymore
certainly
clearly

difinitely
never
nowadays

often
possibly
probably

simply
usually
well

OTHERS

anyway

by the way

great!

than

GRAMMAR

	ONE	BODY	THING	WHERE
SOME	someone	somebody	something	somewhere
ANY	anyone	anybody	anything	anywhere
EVERY	everyone	everybody	everything	everywhere
NO	no one	nobody	nothing	nowhere

GOOD	BETTER (THAN)	THE BEST
BAD	WORSE	WORST
TALL	TALLER	TALLEST
YOUNG	YOUNGER	YOUNGEST
OLD	OLDER	OLDEST
BIG	BIGGER	BIGGEST
SHORT	SHORTER	SHORTEST
SMALL	SMALLER	SMALLEST

ENJOYABLE	MORE ENJOYABLE (THAN)	THE MOST ENJOYABLE
EXCITING	EXCITING	EXCITING
INTERESTING	INTERESTING	INTERESTING
NECESSARY	NECESSARY	NECESSARY
RESTFUL	RESTFUL	RESTFUL
FAMOUS	FAMOUS	FAMOUS

who   how often   what   where   when
                              which   what kind   what

I   usually eat lunch   at that   famous   restaurant on Sunday.

        what   BE how often   how   what

The lunchtime special is usually cheaper than the other lunches.

You   ARE   tired.
You   LOOK   tired.
You   SEEM   tired.

SUMMARY WORD LIST

The number after the word is the number of the lesson in which the word is first used.

a(n) 2
about 2
abbreviation 7
accountant 9
across 4
actually 7
address 7
adjective 7
adverb 10
after 6
afternoon 1
again 3
age 10
ago 7
to agree 4
ahead 3
airport 7
alive 7
all 2
all right 4
almost 3
along 8
alphabet 1
also 7
always 6
and 1
ankle 10
another 4
to answer 1
any 2
anymore 10
anyway 10
anywhere 7
apartment 4
apple 5
to apply 9
April 6
area code 3
arm 10
around 8
as 8
to ask 1
assistance 7
at 1
August 6
aunt 7
avenue 7
away from 8
baby 2
back 1
bad 1
bank 8
bar 9
bathroom 2
to be 1

because 9
bed 10
before 6
to be going to 3
to begin 3
behind 8
to bend 10
beside 8
better/best 10
between 8
big 3
bill 5
Bingo 4
birthday 6
black 2
block 8
blue 2
board 1
book 1
bookkeeper 9
bored 10
born 7
to bother 6
bottom 7
boulevard 7
box 7
boy 2
break 3
breakfast 8
bridge 8
to bring 1
brother 7
brown 2
to brush 10
buck 3
to build 9
building 8
bus 8
business 10
bus stop 8
busy 10
but 3
to buy 4
by 8
by the way 10
cab 9
calendar 6
to call 1
can (mv) 1
car 4
card 2
cashier 9
cassette 5
cat 2
cent 4
center 7
to change 5
channel 3

charge 7
cheap 5
to check 9
chest 10
child(ren) 2
to choose 3
to circle 4
city 7
class 1
classmate 1
classroom 2
clearly 10
clerk 9
(o) clock 6
clothes 4
coffee 5
coin 5
cold 5
to collect 3
color 2
to come 8
to come back 10
company 7
to continue 8
cook 9
corner 7
(in)correct 4
to cost 5
country 3
crowd 10
date 6
daughter 7
day 1
dead 7
December 6
definitely 10
department(dept.) 9
to describe 7
to dial 7
dial tone 7
dictionary 3
to die 7
different 4
difficult 3
dime 5
dinner 8
direction 8
directory 7
to do 1
doctor 9
dog 2
dollar 5
door 3
down 4
downtown 8
to draw 8
to drink 5
to drive 8

driver 9
drug store 8
each 6
ear 10
early 6
east 7
easy 3
to eat 5
eight 3
either 4
elbow 10
elevator 8
eleven 3
else 8
email 9
engineer 9
English 1
enjoyable 9
enough 5
entrance 8
envelope 7
evening 1
every 2
everywhere 2
example 2
excellent 10
exchange 5
exciting 9
to excuse 1
exit 8
expensive 5
experience 9
to explain 9
eye 10
eyebrow 10
face 10
fall (season) 6
family 7
famous 7
far 8
father 7
February 6
to feel 10
(a) few 8
to fill out 9
finally 7
to find 2
to find out 8
fine 1
finger 10
to finish 8
fire station 8
first 1
five 3
to fly 9
to fold 3
to follow 10
food 4

foot 10	if 7	March 6	off 5
for 2	immediately 9	married 7	office 8
to forget 3	in 2	to match 7	often 10
four 3	in back of 8	matter 6	okay 3
Friday 6	inch 10	May 6	old 7
friend 2	information 9	may (mv) 2	on 1
from 1	in front of 8	maybe 6	once 6
fun 9	in person 9	to mean 3	one 1
game 2	inside 7	to meet 9	only 8
to get 4	instruction 7	to mention 5	on time 6
to get dressed 10	interesting 6	middle 7	on top of 8
to get into 8	to interview 9	midnight 6	to open 6
to get off 5	to introduce 9	million 4	operator 7
to get out of 8	January 6	minute 3	or 2
to get to 8	job 4	Miss 7	orange 2
to get up 10	to jog 9	Mister 7	order 10
girl 2	July 6	Monday 6	other 6
to give 2	June 6	money 4	out 3
to go 1	just 4	month 6	outside 7
good 1	kilo 5	more 10	over 1
goodbye 1	knee 10	morning 1	own 7
grammar 1	to know 3	most 6	page 1
grandfather 7	lake 8	mother 7	pair 4
grandmother 7	last 1	mother-in-law 7	paper 3
gray 2	late 3	mouth 10	(news)paper 9
great ! 10	later 1	Mrs. 7	parent 7
green 2	law(yer) 9	Ms. 7	park 8
to guess 4	to learn 4	much 3	partner 7
gym 9	left 5	music 9	to pass 8
hair 10	leg 10	my 1	past 6
half-dollar 5	less 10	name 1	to pay 4
hall 8	lesson 1	near 8	pen 3
hand 5	to let 5	necessary 9	pencil 3
to hand in 3	letter (alphabetic) 1	neck 10	penny 5
to hand out 3	letter 7	to need 5	people 2
to hang up 7	library 8	neither 4	person 2
to happen 3	life/lives 7	(inter)net 9	to pick up 5
to have 2	to like 9	never 10	picture 5
to have got 5	line 7	new 2	piece 3
to have got to 6	lip 10	next 6	pilot 9
to have to 4	(a) little 6	next to 8	pink 2
head 10	little 3	nice 3	place 1
height 10	to lock 3	nickel 5	(air)plane 5
hello 1	long 3	night 6	to play 4
to help 5	to look 1	nine 3	please 1
here 1	to look (seem) 10	no 1	point (decimal) 5
high school 8	to look for 10	nobody 8	to point 1
hip 10	to look like 8	noon 6	police station 8
holiday 6	to look up 3	no one 8	possibly 10
home 1	to lose 3	north 7	postage 4
homework 1	lost 8	nose 10	postal clerk 9
hospital 8	(a) lot 5	not 1	post office 7
hot 5	lottery 3	nothing 6	potato 5
hotel 8	to love 10	noun 7	pound 5
hour 6	lower 7	November 6	practice 1
house 4	lunch 3	now 1	preposition 5
housekeeper 9	main 8	nowadays 10	pretty (quite) 3
how 1	to make 4	number 3	price 5
hundred 4	man/men 2	nurse 9	probably 10
hungry 5	mall 8	October 6	problem 6
husband 7	many 3	of 1	pronunciation 2
to identify 9	map 3	of course 8	province 3

purple 2
to put 5
to put back 5
quarter 5
queer 6
question 2
quite 3
radio 5
rate 5
to read 2
ready 4
really 9
red 2
relative 7
to relax 9
to remember 9
rent 4
to repeat 2
(the) rest 6
restful 9
restaurant 8
to return 7
review 8
rice 5
rich 10
right 1
river 8
road 7
row 4
salt 5
to save 4
sandwich 10
same 10
Saturday 6
to say 1
schedule 1
to seal 7
season 6
seat 1
second 6
second (2nd) 6
to see 1
-self 9
to send 4
sentence 5
September 6
service 10
seven 3
several 7
to shake 10
shopping center 8
short 10
should (mv) 4
shoulder 10
to show 5
shower 10
sick 10
sign 8
simply 10
single 7

sister 7
to sit 3
six 3
to sleep 10
sleepy 10
slowly 1
small 10
so 5
so long 6
some 2
someone 8
sometimes 3
somewhere 10
son 7
sorry 1
soup 10
south 7
to speak 1
special 6
to spell 1
to spend 5
spouse 7
spring (season) 6
stairs 8
stamp 4
to start 8
state 3
station 8
stomach 10
to stop 5
store 9
to straighten 10
street 1
student 1
to study 7
stuff 8
sugar 5
summer 6
Sunday 6
super 10
sure 3
to surf 9
swell 10
to take 3
to talk 7
tall 10
tax 4
taxi 8
tea 5
teacher 1
(tele)phone 3
to tell 4
teller 9
ten 3
than 10
thanks 1
that 1
that 6
the 1
then 3

there 2
there is/are 8
these 2
thing 8
to think 5
third 6
thirsty 5
this 1
those 5
thousand 4
three 2
thumb 10
Thursday 6
ticket 3
time 1
tired 3
to 1
today 5
toe 10
toll-free 7
tomato 5
tomorrow 6
tonight 6
too (also) 2
tooth/teeth 10
top 7
to touch 10
tour 8
tourist 10
toward 8
town 2
toy 9
train station 8
truck 8
true 10
to try 10
Tuesday 6
turn 8
to turn 6
TV 3
twelve 3
twenty 4
twin 7
to twist 10
two 2
to understand 1
uncle 7
until 8
up 4
upper 7
to use 7
usually 10
valley 8
verb 4
very 1
video 9
waist 10
to wait 3
to wait on 10
waiter 9

to walk 8
to want 4
to wash 10
watch 5
to watch 3
Wednesday 6
week 6
weekday 6
weekend 6
to weigh 10
weight 10
welcome 1
well ! 8
well (good) 10
west 7
what 1
whatever 5
when 4
where 1
which 4
(a) while 10
white 2
who 2
whose 5
why 9
wife 7
will (mv) 3
to win 3
winter 6
wired 10
with 2
woman/women 2
word 1
to work 3
to worry 3
worse 10
worth 4
would (mv) 3
would like (to) 9
wrist 10
write 10
wrong 4
yeah 5
year 6
yellow 2
yes 1
yesterday 3
young 10
zero 3
zip code 3
zoo 8
zoo keeper 9